# The
# Success Look —
# For
# Women
# Only

# The Success Look — For Women Only

by Joan K. Dietch

Publishers ● GROSSET & DUNLAP ● New York
A FILMWAYS COMPANY

Illustrations by Barbara Fleischer
Designed by Irene Friedman

Copyright © 1979 by Joan K. Dietch
All rights reserved
Published simultaneously in Canada
Library of Congress catalog card number: 78-067811
ISBN 0-448-16423-X
First printing 1979
Printed in the United States of America

# Acknowledgments —————

My thanks to Alice Edmunds for her professional guidance in putting this material together, and to Pat Fisher for her patience and understanding.

For Joey, who said,
"Mom, I knew you could do it."

# Contents_____

*The
Success Look —
For
Women
Only*

# 1

# Dressing for Success'

Clothing is a form of communication. Our clothes tell a story about *us*, about who we are — or who we think we are or would like to be. Clothing can be a public relations tool for limp egos. Clothes can even serve as a security blanket. They can be sexy, trendy, witty, or boring, but there is no such thing as "just plain clothes." Even a uniform makes a statement.

In the past, a woman's clothes were a visible comment on her husband's status in the community, and women dressed to complement their husbands' images. The Victorians, for instance, believed that *more is more,* and an upper-class Victorian woman took pride in wearing layers of petticoats, a hoop skirt, and a bonnet and in carrying a muff and a parasol. Yet the design and the sheer weight of her outfit helped to restrict her role in her community as effectively as if her feet had been bound.

Today a woman's clothes say as much about her own status and her own identity as the Victorian woman's costume once said about her husband's. By wearing the right clothes, a woman can communicate her own role as a productive member of society. Women are no longer strictly ornamental. We have entered the market place and we are competing with men — and with each other — on every level. It is not enough for a woman, just as it is not enough for a man, to have talent and knowledge and skill — we must also dress for the part.

Women do not have to bury their identities as females, however, to be taken seriously on the job, and we certainly don't have to dress like men in order to be treated as professionals.

The author (male) of one popular book on dressing for success equates dressing like a woman with dressing for failure. And though he says that women shouldn't dress like men, he really means that women shouldn't dress in a man's suit and tie. He does think that women, like men, should be limited to one costume: the woman's success suit — a matching skirt and blazer jacket worn with a blouse of contrasting color.

Who should wear it? Everyone! No matter if a woman is short or tall, fat or thin, no matter what type of job she has or what looks and feels best on her. While some women look good in success suits, other women look like tanks. Dressing by computer doesn't work for everybody — and it doesn't have to work for anybody! There are no hard-and-fast rules on how to dress for work. Some of the sharpest female executives in the country look positively smashing without looking like carbon copies of a man's preconceived idea of how women should dress.

What are some of these preconceived ideas?

Advocates of the success look warn women to avoid sweaters on the job, calling them "lower-middle-class," negative, and fit only for a secretary. Yet pictures taken of Jackie Onassis on the job as an editor show that she wears a sweater and slacks to work. And Diana Vreeland, former editor of both *Vogue* and *Harper's Bazaar,* wears a black cashmere sweater with a black Givenchy skirt to work every day (she has duplicates of each) in the winter and has done so for years. No one ever mistook Diana Vreeland for a secretary.

To look successful, "experts" say a woman cannot have long hair, extra-short hair, or very curly hair. Where does this leave fashion tycoon Diane von Furstenburg, whose thick curls hang halfway down her back? Or, for that matter, where does this leave black women?

Once dressed in the uniform of skirt, matching blazer jacket, and contrasting blouse, the successful woman must remember to keep her jacket on at all times, even when her fellow executives who happen to be male take theirs off. If a woman removes her jacket, she will find herself dressed in a skirt and blouse, an outfit which the "success experts" say is ineffective. But a trim, sleek skirt with a good silk shirt can be one of the most attractive, comfortable, and professional looks for many women.

The successfully dressed woman must remember never to wear her woman's suit to any nonbusi-

13

ness function. In other words, if a woman is going out after work, she must either go home first or change her clothes, à la Clark Kent, in the ladies' room, while her escort waits impatiently in the same suit he wore to work that morning.

Obviously, hard-and-fast rules about how to dress for work were made to be broken, and the sooner the better. A woman can wear whatever she wants to wear to the office — a skirted suit, a pants suit, a skirt and sweater, a dress, even jeans — if the outfit is suitable to her job and if it is neat, clean, well fitting, and in good taste. A woman's sense of authority should come from within, not off a hanger or out of a book.

# It Pays to Know Your Type

I have been studying the psychology of women's clothing for fifteen years, long before women were considered (or considered themselves) to be management material. I've taught thousands of women how to dress to suit their personalities, their figures, and their roles in life. I believed fifteen years ago, as I believe today, that a woman can and should retain her individuality.

Some women have very distinctive personalities and they know exactly how they want to look. They automatically choose the right clothes for themselves to achieve the "look" they are after. But for most women, finding the clothes that look and feel best takes time, money, and divine inspiration.

I would like to help these women to look better at work and spend less. I would like to show them — to show *you* — how to make shopping a pleasure instead of a nightmare. The key is to know your type and to dress consistently. Over the years, most of the women I've advised have fallen into five general types:

## THE EXECUTIVE

She wore the success look before it was "invented." She sticks to the classics: — a tailored suit, a cashmere sweater and a skirt, a blazer and flannel pants — and because the clothes *are* classics, she can wear them year in and year out.

## THE ROMANTIC TYPE

She likes to look more feminine than the woman with the strictly executive look, yet she too wears classic, tailored clothes. She expresses her romantic nature with subtlety, wearing a ruffled blouse under a traditional blazer or a flounced skirt with a man-tailored shirt.

## THE SEDUCTIVE TYPE

Sophia Loren at the office? Why not! Just because a woman has the kind of figure men stare at, she need not count herself out of the job market. The right clothes can give her a look of authority and professionalism without totally eliminating sex appeal.

## THE SOPHISTICATED TYPE

She has *style*. She carries herself with distinction and poise. She wears designer clothes if she can afford them, but anything she wears will look as if it were made for her alone

15

because her personality and self-assurance allow her to wear her individualistic clothes and not the other way around.

## THE INGENUE

Petite, cheerful, forever young, the ingénue must work to offset her little-girl looks if she wants to be taken seriously at work.

In the following chapters, I will give specific advice on what to wear for women of all five types, no matter what their age. By following this advice, any woman can put together more than a wardrobe — she can create an image.

It is important to remember that flexibility is vital to the game of big business and that some situations may call for a change in the kind of image you want to project. When a woman knows her job and knows the people she works with, she can change her type or borrow from other types if it would be to her advantage. A young insurance executive I know found herself working for a man who had filled his office with tennis trophies. Although she had always thought of herself as the executive type, and had always worn silk shirts under her blazers, she made a point of buying a light cotton string V-neck sweater striped at the neck in maroon and navy to look like a tennis sweater, yet with none of a real tennis sweater's bulk, to wear under her blazer for her next meeting with her boss. Perhaps if you work for a man or a woman who is not your type, you can try to change your wardrobe appropriately. Mixing the authoritative colors of the executive with the slightly frilly styles of the romantic could be very effective.

Of course, knowing how to present an authoritative image may help you to get people's attention, but once they are listening to you, you'd better have something to say. All the clothes in the world can't camouflage lack of skill or expertise. Remember, dressing as if you mean business is the easy part!

16

# 2

# The Executive Look _____

> All that you really have to know about fashion is that whatever you're wearing and whatever you are, never let them know that you're afraid.
>
> Eve Babitz

Can wearing simple, tailored, classic clothes really help a woman to climb the corporate ladder of success?

It can't hurt!

The executive look — tailored suits, to be sure, but dresses and blazers and skirts and good wool pants too — is the basic look for ambitious women who work in American offices today, and for good reason. Women wearing the strong, tasteful, almost masculine lines of the executive look exude authority and self-confidence. Their clothes won't ruffle any male egos. In fact, they won't ruffle the egos of female co-workers either. And if wearing well-tailored classic styles can't actually guarantee success on the job, at least they will help a woman to *look* and *feel* successful. The executive look carries with it an aura of success.

Because the executive look is so effective at the office, the clothes that make up this look should be the backbone of any working woman's wardrobe, no matter which type she is. Women of any age can wear these clothes: a younger woman dressed in classic clothes will look mature and capable, while an older woman will be admired for her fine taste, timeless wardrobe, and youthful appearance.

# A New Look for Work

Nancy Fox has been wearing the executive look since she was in college. "I still wear some of the same clothes now that I wore twenty years ago," Nancy told me, "but I wear them mostly on weekends. My old oxford shirts and shetland sweaters are too bulky and too collegiate for the office." After fifteen years at home as a wife and mother, Nancy decided that she wanted to

18

A1

go to law school. Three years later, after she graduated and went to work for a New York City law firm, Nancy found that she wanted a new look for her new life.

On the day I talked to Nancy, she was wearing a dark brown, wool flannel wrap skirt, a silk man-tailored shirt, a soft oatmeal-colored knitted vest which she wore with a narrow, brown leather belt, and a brown tweed blazer (see illustration A1). "I wore this blazer all through law school," Nancy said, "and the vest is older than that, but I bought the shirt and the skirt when I started to work. Most of the clothes I'd worn when I took my children to the park or when I was a student were too casual. I wanted a more 'grown-up' look."

Nancy said that she thought that her wrap skirt was "a little sexy for the office, but the whole outfit is so traditional and conservative that I can get away with it. Besides, it's fun to remind my fellow workers — and myself — that I *am* a woman." Nancy will not allow herself to be limited to one kind of outfit, yet she never loses the executive look with the built-in authority that goes along with it. She feels free to play down the look by wearing something seductive — her wraparound skirt, for instance — yet, by sticking to classic lines and natural fibers, she always looks impeccably right for the office.

Nancy described how she went about choosing a wardrobe for work: "First, I went uptown, to the big department stores on Fifth Avenue, but just to look. I went to three or four different stores, and to a lot of different departments in each store, just to familiarize myself with what was in style and what was available. Then, I went shopping on the Lower East Side, an area full of little shops that sell the same clothes I saw uptown at a discount. As I was already familiar with the current styles, and as I knew what I wanted to buy before I went shopping downtown, it was easy for me to find the clothes I was after. If I couldn't find the actual dress or skirt that I saw uptown, I could find a dress or skirt that resembled it. I bought basic, classic clothes that were made, whenever possible, out of natural fibers. I couldn't afford more than one silk shirt, though, so my other shirts are made of

A2

cotton or synthetic silk blends.

"I was really on the lookout for dresses, since I hadn't worn a dress (except to weddings) for years. I found two that I loved on the Lower East Side, both shirtdresses, one a soft, soft cotton fabric with a pattern that looks like a man's tie (illustration A2), the other in light cotton like a man's shirt that I like to wear with a blazer (illustration A3). Wearing either dress makes me feel *so* feminine."

Wherever you live, you can adapt Nancy's shopping technique to the stores in your area. Check out the best stores in town and then look for a similar style, fabric, and cut in lower-priced and discount stores.

# *The Clothes That Make the Look*

## *DRESSES*

Stock up on the tailored shirtdress, in its endless variations, in as many colors and fabrics and patterns as you can afford. If you can afford to make a major investment, the *ultimate power dress* is the ultrasuede shirtdress. The length of this dress may change from year to year, the style of the collar may be altered, or the sleeves may get fuller or narrower, but the basic line of the dress is still as classic and pure as it was when the dress was introduced by Halston in 1972 — at $180. The dress was a smash hit with successful women and the ambitious women who emulated them. Actually, at $180, the dress would have been a good investment. Now the ultrasuede shirtdress sells — like hotcakes — for around $400.

If, like Nancy Fox, you can't afford ultrasuede, choose shirtdresses in soft cottons, either in solid colors or in traditional, conservative patterns.

A3

## SUITS

There's nothing basically *wrong* with the success suit, which is a matching skirt and blazer jacket. The success suit can make a woman look as serious and as capable as a man, but there is no reason why a woman should be limited to this look.

Within the success look itself there is plenty of room for individual expression. It is possible, as shown in illustration A4, to soften the look by wearing a sweater under the jacket with a scarf knotted at the throat instead of wearing a more severely tailored blouse.

If you'd like to lighten the look of a skirted suit, try a suit with a shorter jacket. As seen in illustration A5, it's a young, fresh look, yet just as right for the office as its more traditional forebear.

## SEPARATES

If you've shopped wisely, you were already on your way to a closet full of wearable separates when you brought your suits home. You'll be able to wear the jackets with other skirts and with pants, and you'll be able to wear the skirts with any number of shirts, sweaters, and other jackets.

The idea with separates is that everything should be able to be worn with everything else, giving you the maximum number of clothing combinations. Coordinating a wardrobe like that isn't easy — you mst have a very firm idea of what clothes you already have when you go shopping for new clothes — but once you've done it, you can practically dress in the dark and still come out looking like an executive vice-president, or, at the very least, an executive trainee.

The basic parts of a wardrobe of separates are:

### BLAZER JACKETS

Buy them in solid colors and in tweeds. Ideally, they should be made of good wool or wool flannel in the winter and

A4

A5

of linen in the summer. If you must buy a blazer made of synthetic, try to find one in a synthetic *blend* with the look of natural fibers. Blazers don't go out of style — you can wear a blazer forever — so it might be worth it to pay a little more to get the real thing. In illustration A6, the traditional blazer is shown layered with a man-tailored shirt and a sweater.

## SHIRTS

Man-tailored shirts will *never* go out of style, whether they are made of silk, a synthetic silklike blend, or cotton. Wear them in solid colors, as seen in illustration A5, or in a conservative pattern, as seen in illustration A7.

## SWEATERS

Stick to the basics when it comes to style. If you are after variety, you can buy the basic styles — turtlenecks (illustration A4), cowl-necks (illustrations A6 and A7), or basic jewel necklines — in as many colors and wools (cashmere, lamb's wool, etc.) as you can afford. Sweater vests, like the one in illustration A1, are also a good investment and a wonderful way to keep warm and look "pulled together" at the same time.

## SKIRTS

Once again, stick to the classics — the gathered dirndl, the A-line, the narrow slim skirt — and express your individuality through color and pattern. But if you plan to wear blouses and/or blazers with patterns and tweeds, most of your skirts (and pants) should be solid-colored.

## PANTS

*Of course* you can wear pants to work, *if:*

1. You look good in pants. Long, lean bodies look good

A6

A7

in pants. If you look better in a skirt, why not look better?

2. The women with clout in your company wear pants. If not, you still may choose to wear pants, but you may find yourself becoming more of a crusader than a corporate success.

Pants look great with a shirt and a blazer, as in illustration A8, or with a simple jewel neckline sweater and scarf, as seen in illustration A9.

# *The Look to Avoid*

Think like a man, work like a man, earn a salary like a man, but never, *never* dress like a man! (See illustration A10.) Why look like a second-rate man when you can look like a first-rate woman!

# *Colors, Fabrics, and Patterns*

The woman in the gray flannel suit? Why not! The woman who wears the executive look wears a lot of dark colors: gray, brown, and dark muted green are favorites. But her clothes are so tailored and her appearance so authoritative that she can also wear neutral beiges and lighter colors such as yellow and powder blue without losing her air of confidence. In fact, wearing

A8

A9

*THE LOOK TO AVOID*                    A10

softer shades may help to tone down an image that is too severe, and will keep an executive woman from overwhelming her co-workers.

Whenever possible, the executive woman wears clothes made of natural fibers — cotton, linen, silk, and wool. Clothing made of the real thing can be (much) more expensive and (much) harder to wash or dry clean than synthetics, but it is usually worth the investment and the effort for the look and all-around durability of natural fibers.

You don't have to stick to solid colors to wear this look, but if you do want to buy a shirt or jacket or skirt with a pattern, keep it simple and keep it traditional. British tweeds are beautiful, foulards and paisleys are very effective, and, of course, a conservative stripe or a tattersall plaid always looks good.

# *The Mature Woman and the Executive Look*

A dynamite combination!

The classic lines of the executive look can be especially complimentary to the mature woman. Though the clothes are ageless and timeless, if you are a mature woman you will look younger in neat, trim, classic styles. Take a hint from the great French designer, Coco Chanel, who pioneered the relaxed classic look:

"A young girl can get away with throwing on any old rag; an older woman has to have clothes of superior cut and fabric. What counts is neatness, neatness, neatness. Sloppiness adds years."

34

# 3

# *The Romantic Look*—————————

"No matter what the occasion," Yvette Neilson said to me, "and no matter how serious and businesslike I must look, I've always tried to add a feminine touch to my outfit. It's just my romantic nature coming out, I guess."

At fifty-five years old, Yvette Neilson is one of the most respected and experienced buyers in Chicago. By now, it comes as second nature to Yvette to choose and order the styles that will sell from the thousands of styles made by the two-hundred-odd clothing manufacturers that make up Yvette's "market."

"I'm out in the morning two or three times a week, visiting manufacturers, and I make buying trips to New York and California four times a year. I also attend fashion shows. When I am here in my office, manufacturer's representatives are in and out all day. And, since we're all in the business, we all notice each other's clothes."

Yvette Neilson certainly looked like a serious, successful businesswoman the day we spoke in her busy office at one of Chicago's finest department stores. Yvette was wearing a classic wool suit in a conservative British-looking tweed and a light wool sweater-vest (illustration B1). But she added her personal signature to this masculine, executive look when she added a patterned silk shirt with an ultrafeminine, big, floppy bow.

"I've been in the fashion business for thirty years," Yvette told me. "When I was younger, I wore every far-out style the designers could dream up. Wearing the latest style was important to me both personally and professionally. After all, as a buyer, I'm constantly on display to the rest of the fashion world. But now that I'm fifty-five, I've gotten much more conservative in my dress habits. I tend to avoid fads and wear classic businesslike clothes. I'm always wearing suits and blazers and shirtdresses these days. I always add my own bright, feminine touch, however — a ruffle here, a bow there, or maybe just a touch of delicate lace — to these conservative styles."

Yvette spoke out strongly against the "fashion tyranny" of the success look promoted by male dress experts. "My daughter is getting her master's degree in business in graduate school, and her professors — men, naturally — tell her and her classmates that they *must* wear a conservative suit with a conservative shirt to be taken seriously as executive material. Sure, that outfit looks good, but so do other outfits. My daughter, who is a buxom five-feet-tall, looks like a pouter pigeon in a costume like that. She needs to wear something softer, less masculine. Yet it is all I can do — and I am in the fashion business — to convince her to dress like the woman she is rather than the neutered executive her professors think she should become."

B1

I hope Yvette's daughter listens to her mother, not her professors. She couldn't pick a better example of a woman who looks pretty *and* efficient. Yvette Neilson looks romantic in her ruffles and bows, yet she projects authority.

# *The Clothes That Make the Look*

## *DRESSES*

The shirtdress, of course, is the basic dress of any working woman's wardrobe. Women who consider themselves romantics adapt this look to their own sensibility, however. A woman could look romantic in a feminine version of a shirtdress, yet still look perfectly acceptable at work. The dress shown in illustration B2, for instance, has many romantic touches: the fabric itself, a soft, silky synthetic blend, the color, a soft peach, and the detail work, the tiny tucks, the gathered waist, the bow at the waist. Yet the line of the dress is as classic as the line of the executive woman's shirtdress.

## *SUITS*

The cut is classic, but the detail is feminine. Shown in illustration B3, three classic success suits are accessorized for a woman with a romantic bent with soft blouses complete with bows and ruffles. Pretty? Yes. Efficient? Of course!

The trick here is all in the artful use of color and fabric. The same suit that looks masculine and businesslike in banker's gray looks very feminine, but just as businesslike, in lilac or in bright pink. The shirts, which might look too frilly for the office in pastels, look authoritative in deep tones of gray or burgundy.

B2

*B3*

B4

B5

B6

*B7*

## *SEPARATES*

To wear clothes that are romantic yet properly businesslike takes very careful planning when putting together a wardrobe of separates. A romantic tiered skirt can look wonderful, a frilly blouse can look wonderful, a lacy shawl can look wonderful, but if you wear them all together, *you'll* look dreadful. Remember to balance your romantic clothes by wearing them with conservative, executive-look clothes.

## *BLAZER JACKETS*

There's nothing romantic about a blazer. You can put a blazer over a blouse with both ruffles and a bow (illustration B4), and you're dressed for a board meeting. You may wear blazers with even your most extravagantly romantic separates. In illustration B5, for instance, the lacy shawl *and* the tiered skirt would look too feminine for office wear, but the executive-look blazer adds just the right sober, serious touch to this otherwise whimsical outfit.

## *SHIRTS*

The more feminine the style of the blouse, the more authoritative that blouse's color should be. Frilly, ruffly blouses that look marvelous in glossy dark brown (see illustration B6) would look too sweet and girlish in pastel pink.

## *SWEATERS*

Here's a good way to let your romantic nature shine through. Wearing soft, feminine sweaters like the one shown in illustration B7 is fine for the office as long as the romantic look is played down by mixing the sweater with a classic conservative skirt. On the other hand, you can wear a classic executive-look sweater with a romantic flowered skirt, as shown in illustration B8, and still look the capable businesswoman that you are.

45

## *SKIRTS*

The tiered skirt shown in illustration B5 has been an American fashion staple for years. Award-winning designer Ralph Lauren featured this skirt as one of the designs in his recent romantic frontier collection. Worn with a conservative blazer, this skirt can look as good in the office as it looks in the corral.

A basic, classic skirt (illustration B7) mixes well with a romantic top. A woman wearing this combination can look romantic without losing anyone's professional respect and admiration.

The skirts shown in illustrations B8 and B9 mix classic cut with a romantic pattern. Worn with tailored clothes, however, these skirts acquire just the right touch of authority.

## *PANTS*

The same rules apply as for the executive look: wear pants if they look good on you and if other women in your company wear pants. Your pants, like your blazer, should be a balancing conservative element in your wardrobe. Stick to the basic good wools and linens of the executive wardrobe when it comes to wearing pants, and save your romantic flights of fancy for your blouses, sweaters, skirts, and accessories.

# *The Look to Avoid*

Never mix a romantic top with a romantic skirt without wearing something — a blazer, for instance — to turn the feminine romantic look into a capable businesslike look (illustration B10).

46

B8

B9

*THE LOOK TO AVOID*                                                    *B10*

# *Colors, Fabrics, and Patterns*

Be very careful with colors. If you want to wear romantic pale pastels, your clothes must be cut along simple, classic lines. Conversely, wear feminine frilly styles only in strong, authoritative, masculine colors.

Clothing made of frilly, lacy fabrics must be counterbalanced in any outfit by clothing made of more conservative fabrics. The lacy scarf in illustration B5 that looks so smashing against a wool blazer would look silly if it were worn with an equally lacy blouse.

A flowered skirt, like the one in illustration B8, is only right for the office when it is coordinated with an otherwise conservative outfit.

# *The Mature Woman and the Romantic Look*

Yvette Neilson thinks that the romantic look is the most flattering look for a mature woman, and she dresses accordingly. The neat, clean lines of classically tailored clothing softened by a feminine ruffle or bow can be very flattering to most women, but perhaps flatters the mature woman most of all.

# 4

# *The Seductive Look*_____

*To really seduce, you must never be too sure of yourself;
or overly emphatic.*

Lady Emerald Cunard

_____

"What I wear isn't as important to me professionally as it is personally," Juliette Reed told me in her book-lined office in Boston. "In some jobs," Juliette continued, "a woman can wear whatever she wants to wear to work. I have a friend who works as a commercial photographer. One day she'll wear blue jeans and hiking boots, the next she'll be dressed as a gypsy. We're not *that* far-out in publishing, but the clothes I wear to the office, and the clothes I see other women wearing at the office, wouldn't work at a bank or at IBM. We're very individualistic here, and, in most cases (though not in mine), very casual. Most of the younger women think nothing of wearing jeans to the office — well-cut French jeans, to be sure, but jeans none the less. I don't wear jeans myself, though, because I try to wear clothes that fall softly on my body without defining it.''

At forty-two years old, Juliette Reed is a senior editor at a prestigious publishing house. She is a striking woman to look at, tall and full-figured — the kind of woman men notice. "With my body, I have to be careful that my clothes don't stand out. I try to look conservative, but no matter how conservative my outfit, I can't and won't hide the fact that I am a woman. I've learned to wear softer clothes, clothes which are more flattering to my figure than the more severe executive look.''

On the day we met, Juliette was dressed beautifully in a soft, flowing brown suit (illustration C1) worn with a glossy shirt in a deeper brown. The lines of the suit were simple and classic, the color was businesslike — what was different, what made the suit so seductive and womanly, was the *fabric:* soft wool crepe, unlined and unconstructed. The whole outfit moved when Juliette moved, falling on her body, yet flowing around it at the same time. Everything was suggested, but nothing was defined. This fluid look is the secret to dressing a woman so she looks capable and efficient while still looking seductive.

"I feel especially elegant in this outfit," Juliette told me, "and I try to wear it when we have meetings of the editorial board or when I'm going out to lunch with a particularly distinguished author. But one of my authors is a hippie who lives on an ashram in California. When I go to lunch with her, I wear a more understated outfit. I try to dress appropriately and well.''

Juliette emphasizes that her style of dressing is very per-

C1

sonal, and that not everyone in publishing dresses the way she does. "I see editorial assistants coming to work for us straight from college. Some of them — the ones that can afford it — look like a page out of *Vogue,* and others wear sober, sensible suits every single day. I think they will learn that what they wear has little bearing on their careers here. In publishing, we care about what's inside someone's head, not what's inside her closet. Looking neat and well-dressed can't hurt, of course, but nobody here gets a promotion because of the way she looks."

# *The Clothes That Make the Look*

### DRESSES

The shirtwaist dress shown in illustration C2 is cut fuller than the dresses shown in earlier chapters. The gathers on the shoulders and the soft, flowing sleeves are more feminine — more *womanly* — than the severely man-tailored dresses worn by the woman with the executive look. The line is uncluttered and unfussy. The fabric, a fluid wool jersey, is sensuous, while the color, conservative banker's gray, works at the office.

The shirtwaist can also look good on a woman with a seductive figure when it skims over the body in a long, silky fall. The shirtdress shown in illustration C3 is *almost* man-tailored, making it even more feminine.

Yet another variation of the shirtwaist is shown in illustration C4. This dress is loose and draped, not tight-fitting or obviously sexy.

*Nothing* is more becoming to a seductive woman than a sweater, of course, and this lamb's wool, cowl-necked sweater

C2

C3

C4

dress (illustration C5) could be wonderful for a cold day. Be careful about fit, though. Nothing you wear should be tight, and that goes double for a sweater.

## SUITS

Wearing loose, flowing suits that move when you do, suits that are distant cousins indeed to the structured, staid success suit, is a good way for a seductive woman to appear as professional as possible. Remember, the idea is not to mask your figure but to show it off in the best possible way. The suit Juliette Reed wore to work on the day we met (illustration C1) is a perfect example.

## SEPARATES

The same fluid look that Juliette Reed likes in suits is reflected in her separates. "When I discovered Harriet Selwyn's Fragments," Juliette told me, "I knew I had found a designer who makes clothes with a woman like me in mind. When a woman finds a designer who is really on her wavelength, she should stick with her. So what if all your clothes look alike — in some circles, that's known as *style*."

Harriet Selwyn is a designer from California who designs one-size-fits-all, everything-goes-with-everything-else separates for a company called Fragments. You can mix, match, or layer the different pieces for an unfussy look. Everything is soft and flowing. A little shopping around should turn up other pieces by different manufacturers which you can turn into your own mix-and-match wardrobe.

## BLAZER JACKETS

It is not as easy to play down a soft, fluid outfit by adding a blazer as it is to play down a romantic shirt or skirt. In fact, a

C5

loose-fitting blazer could look very unflattering on a woman with a full figure. When Juliette Reed wears a blazer, it is fitted close to the body — not tight, but fitted (illustration C6).

## SHIRTS

Again, unfussy should be the key word when it comes to shirts. The shirts shown in illustration C7 and C8 are soft and womanly, but because of their uncluttered lines, they are perfectly acceptable for office wear, especially when worn with easy, understated skirts.

## SWEATERS

If they are flattering, and if they are *not tight,* sweaters are ideal for the office, but the simpler the better should be the rule. Cowl-neck sweaters are terribly flattering. For a change from the basic wool sweater, try wearing a velour top. The V-necked velour sweater shown in illustration C9 would look best in a deep, conservative color.

## SKIRTS

A fluid, soft skirt looks beautiful at the office as long as the cut is simple, the color is businesslike, and as long as it fits. Wear these fluid skirts with soft, sensuous tops. Don't try to play them down by wearing a tailored blazer. It just won't work. But you can wear a classic executive shirt with a soft, flowing skirt, and the combination will work beautifully.

## PANTS

The same advice holds true for pants as it does for sweaters: wear simple, classic pants if they are flattering and if they are not tight.

C6

C7

C8

C9

*THE LOOK TO AVOID*                                    *C10*

# *The Look to Avoid*

The form-fitting leotard look, though wonderful for discos or dance class, does not belong in an office, assuming it's promotions you want and not propositions. (See illustration C10.)

# *Colors, and Fabrics, Patterns*

Keep away from bright colors that would call attention to what you are wearing. Wearing red or orange or bright blue could label you the office femme fatale. Charcoal gray, navy blue, and various shades of brown — underplayed executive colors — should be your choices for work.

Soft, fluid fabrics that follow the body but do not cling are the best fabrics you can wear at the office. When you are wearing classic skirts or pants, wearing a sensuous dark satin or velour top will look womanly without being blatantly sexy. Some men — and some women — are afraid that an aggressively sexy woman will use her sexuality to get ahead on the job. To look seductive and look efficient at the same time takes great subtlety.

Women whose bodies call attention to their clothes should not wear clothing that calls attention to itself. Stick to dark, solid colors for the office.

66

# *The Mature Woman and the Seductive Look*

All those flowing clothes could look frumpy and sloppy on a mature woman. Neatly fitted clothes look far more flattering.

D1

# 5

## *The Sophisticated Look*

*To have style, you must truly believe in yourself.*
Yves Saint Laurent

---

"Most of the women who sell real estate around here wear triple-knit polyester pants suits. I don't," Dorothy Kane said emphatically as we sat and talked in her real estate office in a picturesque New England town. "We're only three hours from New York," she continued, "and only two and a half hours from Boston, so most of my clients are city people. I have found that dressing like a sophisticated New York career women gives my big-city customers confidence in me."

The outfit Dorothy wore that day would have inspired confidence in the heart of any corporate executive. She looked stunning in a matching skirt and tunic top in a soft jersey with a silk scarf knotted under the tunic's loose V-neck and a narrow belt at the waist. "I'm wearing high-heeled shoes now," Dorothy said, "but if I get a call to show a country property, I'll change to the boots I keep in the car.

"I find it hard to find the sophisticated clothes I like in town," Dorothy told me, "so I do most of my shopping in bulk in New York City. But whenever I find anything that looks like me, I buy it, no matter where I see it, whether I need it or not. That's the only way to build a really personal wardrobe. It never works for me to shop for a specific item. I just wear what I have and buy things when I find them."

What makes a woman like Dorothy Kane sophisticated is the way everything she wears looks as if it were made for her alone. She imparts her personal style to all her outfits. She wears clothes with simple lines and adds her own touches — in this case, the scarf and the belt (illustration D1).

Sophisticated clothes are just a bit *different,* a bit more stylized than other clothes. To wear them, a woman must be supremely sure of herself. She must carry herself with poise and distinction. But she must also take special care that her attitude toward her co-workers is never condescending or threatening, or she will find herself very unpopular at work.

# *The Clothes That Make the Look*

## *DRESSES*

The shirtwaist dress can look *very* sophisticated and still look efficient and businesslike at work. For example, the collar-

D2

D3

D4

less neckline and blouson waist of the shirtdress in illustration D2 help this basic dress to look more than basic. And the pared-down elegance of the shirtdress in illustration D3 makes for an equally sophisticated image.

## SUITS

The look here is more elegant than in earlier chapters. What's personal and different about the suit in illustration D4 is the cut of the jacket — short and boxy with wide, slightly padded shoulders. A soft silk, patterned blouse is worn under the jacket. Could *you* wear a patterned blouse with a checked jacket? A sophisticated woman can wear anything and feel and look great in it!

## SEPARATES

The cut of your separates and the individual way you wear them are the secrets of sophisticated mixing and matching.

### BLAZER JACKETS

A long, narrow blazer, as seen in illustration D5, is much more sophisticated than the classic executive blazer, and will make a basic executive shirt and skirt look sophisticated too.

Another way to wear a blazer is to wrap it loosely around the body and belt it at the waist. A woman dressed in the outfit shown in illustration D6 or in illustration D7 looks smart, capable, businesslike, *and* stylish — what a combination!

### SHIRTS

The classic, understated silk shirts of the executive look are perfect under a sophisticated blazer. Can a silk shirt look sophisticated on its own? That same classic look is pared down to

D5

D6

D7

*D8*

D9

its essentials and shown with a shawl collar in illustration D8 — very sophisticated, but businesslike, too.

## SWEATERS

Only the simplest of sweaters worn with either a scarf or a string of pearls really looks sophisticated. Take your inspiration from fashion wizard Diana Vreeland, who wears a classic black cashmere sweater all winter and looks positively smashing.

## SKIRTS

Once again, the idea is to keep your skirt simple and pared down so as not to distract from your total look. Skirts really aren't sophisticated — it's all in how you wear them and what you wear with them.

## PANTS

Of course pants can look sophisticated at the office — Jackie Onassis looks marvelous in hers, and no one has ever taken her for a member of the typing pool. A sophisticated pants look is shown in illustration D9. This pants suit, with its pleated pants, easy-fitting vest, and unfitted and unstructured jacket is *nothing* like the "triple-knit polyesters" that Dorothy Kane avoids wearing.

# The Look to Avoid

The outfit shown in illustration D10 is *too* sophisticated for work. Be careful not to overdress. Remember — you're going to work, not to a cocktail party.

*THE LOOK TO AVOID*

D10

# Colors, Fabrics, and Patterns

Dark colors are right for office wear, but the sophisticated woman can wear any color and carry it off. Some of her favorite outfits are in light, neutral colors, and she loves black, white, and black and white. Most of her outfits are monochromatic, or at least color-keyed to look subtle, so as not to detract from the simplicity of her clothing. Pastels are out of the question for a true sophisticate.

Natural fibers are the most sophisticated. A heavy British tweed would be too sporty for a sophisticated woman — she prefers light, sheer wools, jerseys, and silks.

Although the most sophisticated clothes come in solid colors, the sophisticated woman also likes to mix different patterns together. If done wrong, the look that results is too busy. If done right, it can be breathtakingly bold.

# The Mature Woman and the Sophisticated Look

If she has a long, lean body, the mature woman can look even more sophisticated when dressed right than her younger female co-workers. Actually, it is easier for a mature woman to look sophisticated than it is for the younger woman. Over the years, many women develop and perfect their own styles so that it comes as second nature to wear basic, pared-down clothes with the personal touch that spells sophistication.

82

# 6

## *The Ingénue Look* _____

"I think many women in business, no matter how tall or how small, have trouble being taken seriously by men — professionally, that is. But I'm only five feet tall, and I think I have more trouble than most. I've had bosses who preferred patting me on the top of my head to giving me a promotion."

Gail Webb is the perfect ingénue. She is tiny, delicate, and, in the words of Bob Dylan, "forever young." "I'm flattered when people think I'm ten years younger than I really am," Gail told me. "Any thirty-three-year-old woman would be. But it's *not* flattering to be treated like a little girl instead of the mature, capable businesswoman that I am. One of my tricks is to always try to meet new business associates while I'm sitting behind my desk. Another is to wear clothes that make me look self-confident. I find that people tend to have more confidence in me if I look and act sure of myself.''

Gail produces television commercials for a Los Angeles advertising agency. "I'm only in my office two or three days a week," Gail said. "The rest of the time I'm out at a film studio or on location somewhere. I used to dress very casually when I went out on a "shoot," but I learned that wearing jeans and a sweatshirt did not enhance my credibility, so now I dress in tailored clothes no matter where I work. Clothes like that give me more presence, which, at five feet, I can certainly use.

"At this agency," Gail told me, "you can almost tell what a woman's job is by the clothes she wears. Women who work as account executives dress very conservatively. The casual look is *out* for them — they wear dresses one hundred percent of the time. Women who work as copywriters dress like conservative businesswomen when they meet with their clients, but they dress very casually when they work with other creative people from the agency. Women from the art department tend to wear blue jeans a lot of the time."

The day we talked at her office, Gail was dressed in a classic, gray wool skirt, a gray, soft cotton, tailored blouse and a gray V-neck sleeveless sweater vest, and she wore a soft, gray plaid blazer to complete the outfit (illustration E1). "I wear a lot of vests," Gail said. "I think a vest makes an outfit more important somehow. I got this one in the boys' department," she added with a smile. "As long as I stick to the most classic, tailored styles, I can find a lot of clothes in the children's department. I have to be careful, though, not to come out looking like a schoolgirl.

"Shopping can be a problem for women like me who are hard to fit," Gail said, "especially if you're on a budget and can't afford to have everything altered. Over the years, I've learned which stores are likely to have something in my size, and going

84

E1

there first cuts down on my shopping time. I've also discovered that imported French or Italian clothes are cut much smaller than American clothes. In general, I look for clothes which have the classic lines of the executive look, but the clothes must be scaled down for my small-boned frame. I get lost in heavy shapes and heavy fabrics.''

The ingenue is perhaps the most difficult image to deal with if you want to turn yourself into executive material — and, happily, the type that can benefit most from wearing the right clothes, clothes which play down a youthful appearance and suggest competence and expertise. Your wardrobe can be the single most important element in helping you out of the "little girl" mold.

# *The Clothes That Make the Look*

## *DRESSES*

The ingénue should strive for the most tailored look she can achieve. However, in choosing tailored, simple clothes, it is important that the ingénue avoid an overly severe or mannish appearance. Because of her diminutive size, looking masculine could make her look just as "cute" as if she were wearing ruffles and frills.

The sweater shirtdress in illustration E2 has a soft, delicate look about it that is appropriate for a petite woman, yet tailored for office wear.

Another shirtdress that would look especially good on a small woman is shown in illustration E3. The raised waistline gives this dress a delicate Empire look that is so flattering to a tiny figure, while the traditional yet delicate dark paisley pattern gives authority to an ingenue's youthful image.

E2

E3

E4

## SUITS

Large, bulky, traditional success suits are wrong for the ingénue. Her suits must be proportioned to fit her smaller body. The suit in illustration E4 with its short jacket and close-to-the-body yet easy fit has the proper proportions for an ingénue and is just as appropriate as the success suit for the business world.

## SEPARATES

Wearing a vest adds authority to an outfit and gives it a finished look. A woman who wants to enhance her credibility as a serious, mature businesswoman should invest in a variety of vests — vests to wear with shirtdresses, with skirts, with shirts, and under jackets.

### BLAZER JACKETS

The classic executive blazer looks good on an ingenue if it is proportioned to fit, and if it is made of a lightweight — never bulky — fabric. Unless you are very slim, however, a hip-length blazer, while high on the authority scale, is likely to make a short woman look broad and dumpy rather than smartly efficient.

### SHIRTS

The blouse in illustration E5 with its feminine yet tailored self-tie is simple, elegant, and stylish. Worn with a conservative plaid vest and a simple, classic skirt, the outfit looks right in any office situation.

### SWEATERS

The V-neck sweater in illustration E6 is perfect for the ingenue's business wardrobe. It is made of light wool, which makes it soft, and it is cut close to the body. A small woman must take care that she doesn't get lost in her clothes, and she could

E5

*E6*

E7

easily get lost in a large, bulky sweater with a big turtleneck or cowl neck.

## SKIRTS

Keep the style classic, keep the line in proportion and easy — no tiny, tight skirts and no voluminous skirts either — and keep the hemline just below the knee. A longer skirt will make the ingénue look dowdy and a shorter skirt will make her look too young and cute. The easy-fitting, soft wool skirt shown in illustration E6 is perfect for a small woman.

Matching a vest to an easy-fitting skirt, as in illustration E7, looks conservative and pulled-together, which is the best way to look at work. In addition, the vertical stripes add height because they pull the eye upward.

## PANTS

Wearing pants to work can be tricky for the ingénue. Great care must be taken to avoid looking like a little man. Adding a soft vest — not a stiff wool vest — and a soft scarf tied loosely at the neck (illustration E8) helps.

# The Look
# to Avoid

The schoolgirl look, shown in illustration E9, is much too collegiate for the office. If you look like a little girl, you can't dress like a little girl.

"Big dresses," as in illustration E10, are just too much dress for the ingenue. Small women must pay special attention to proportion and fit or they will look sloppy, and sloppy women look neither capable nor promotable.

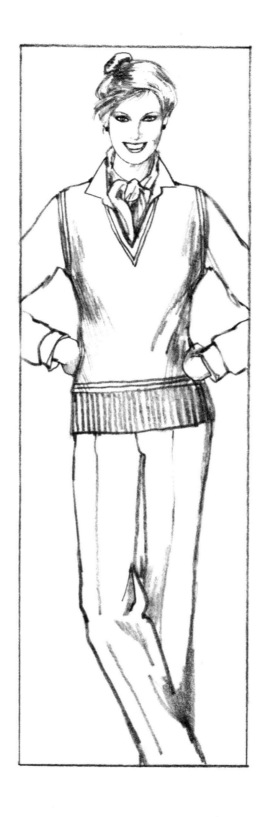

*E8*

E9                    *THE LOOK TO AVOID*

*THE LOOK TO AVOID*                                        *E10*

# Colors, Fabrics, and Patterns

Dark, authoritative colors are the only answer for the ingénue who wants to be taken seriously. Navy, black, and various shades of gray should be the mainstay of her wardrobe. Avoid wearing pastels during business hours. White, powder blue, and beige are generally looked on as "serious" colors, however, and may be used as accent colors.

The ingénue's clothes should be made of soft, light fabrics. Sheer wools (and by sheer I don't mean transparent, I mean lightweight) are perfect. Anything too heavy could look bulky and awkward.

If the ingenue wears patterns, they should be traditional and on a small scale. A large print would be overwhelming on a petite woman.

# The Mature Woman and the Ingénue Look

Fifty years old and still a size five? Good for you! You know by now that you must *always* appear smartly dressed and well groomed, for, at your age, sloppy could turn into frumpy. To look like someone's boss instead of someone's grandmother, you must maintain a strictly tailored image and a trim figure.

# 7

## Finishing Touches: Accessories, Fabrics, How to Shop, and Other Helpful Tips for the Success Look____

## Accessories

What you wear *with* your clothes can make or break your outfit.

## SHOES

Your shoes should enhance, not detract from, the businesslike image you project. The basic pump with a closed toe and heel is still the best shoe for a working wardrobe. Good-looking, plain leather or suede boots — not hiking boots, snow boots, cowboy boots, or motorcycle boots — are perfectly acceptable for office wear in cool or cold weather. When the weather is warm, the open-back, T-strap shoe is cool, comfortable, and neatly impressive. But save the open-toe look, heavy platform soles, ankle straps, and sandals for after five o'clock.

## *HANDBAGS*

No other accessory in your wardrobe stands out the way your handbag does. It must be kept spotless inside and out. For business dress, carry a good leather bag that will coordinate with most of your clothes. A neutral luggage-brown bag will probably look good with everything you own. Your handbag should be large enough to carry all your personal items, but make sure your bag never gets so huge that it is heavy and unwieldy.

Can a woman carry both a handbag and a briefcase for her papers? Why not! When choosing your briefcase, however, keep in mind the style and color of your handbag.

## *GLOVES*

When buying gloves, always buy the best leather you can afford. Vinyl doesn't last and becomes stiff in cold weather. A good pair of leather, fur-lined gloves in basic shades of brown or black will go with everything and keep your hands toasty warm through several winters.

## *SCARVES*

Scarves are an inexpensive way to add versatility to an

office wardrobe, but there are certain dos and don'ts to re-member. If you have a short neck, a scarf tied down near the breastbone adds length while a scarf tied around your neck choker-style leaves you with no neck at all. If your neck is long and thin, it is more flattering to tie your scarf around your neck. The mature woman should know that scarves are great for cov-ering crepy skin.

## JEWELRY

There is one short rule for jewelry in the office — keep it simple and of good quality. One 14-karat gold chain is worth all the junk jewelry you can buy. If you cannot afford to buy good jewelry, it is better to wear none at all. Wearing junk jewelry with an expensive outfit doesn't make the jewelry look good, it makes the outfit look cheap.

What jewelry should you wear? Even if it's real, wear as little as possible. Small gold or silver earrings are always accept-able in the office. One string of pearls looks lovely. One or two gold chains are fine, but bracelets must be worn with care. One good, gold or silver bracelet can look attractive and effective, but never wear more than one at a time, and never wear even one if that bracelet is noisy. Nothing is worse and more distracting than the sound of someone's bracelets clanking. (Well, maybe some-one cracking chewing gum is worse.)

Before wearing a bracelet, or, for that matter, any piece of jewelry to the office, try it on and look at yourself in a full-length mirror. If there is any doubt in your mind about your jewelry, save it for nights and weekends, but don't wear it to work. In fact, if you have any doubts about what you are wearing, change. After all, how can you look like a confident, capable business-woman if you don't feel like one?

## HATS

The days when no woman was well-dressed without a hat are long gone. Unless you feel hats are essential to expressing your individuality and personal style, you should choose them carefully and wear them only in the proper season. Most spring and summer hats look frivolous and out-of-place in business situations. For fall, a small brimmed hat can look both chic and businesslike. In the winter, stay away from little-girl knit caps — those ski-slope creations featuring tassels and pompons. A close-cut fur cloche looks smart and is great for keeping your ears warm, and again, a good-looking brimmed hat is always neat and businesslike.

## HAIR

Your hairstyle must be coordinated with your overall appearance and your personality type. Long blonde curls on a statuesque, sophisticated woman can be elegant; the same style might make a tiny woman look like Alice in Wonderland. Whatever style you feel most comfortable in, make sure it is well cut, simple, and easy to care for.

Should a woman color gray hair? Why not! But again, it's a personal decision based on your appearance and how you feel about yourself. Many woman look elegant, dignified and authoritative with gray hair. The main thing to remember about coloring your hair — whether you're covering gray, enhancing it, or changing your hair color entirely — is to get a professional treatment. Your hair makes a major contribution to your image and it pays to spend a little money for a professional job.

## COATS

Unless you are able to afford a number of coats, your winter coat and your raincoat should be basic enough to go over everything you wear to work. A classic, tan trench-style raincoat will never go out of style (to look like a spy — or a fashion model — *tie* the belt instead of putting it through the buckle). A basic wrap coat in camel or gray wool fits over blazers as well as blouses and will never clash with whatever you're wearing. Not only that — wrap coats look more efficient than any other style.

# *Fabrics*

In this age of synthetics, it is easy to become spoiled by clothes which can go into the washer and the dryer and never need to be ironed. But ease of care is not the only thing to consider when choosing fabrics for business wear. You should also think about a fabric's ability to breathe, how long it will last, and how good it looks.

Polyester is one of the most popular fabrics on the market today. The easiest of easy-care fabrics, it is so popular that it has become a cliché. Pastel polyester pants suit parades can be seen every day at the supermarket and the laundromat, which is reason enough to keep polyester out of the office. There are other reasons too, though. Polyester doesn't breathe — it causes and holds perspiration, which is not an asset in close office quarters. On top of that, polyester wrinkles and it feels like a Brillo pad when one sits on it for any length of time.

Natural fabrics such as cotton and wool may cost more to buy and more to keep clean, but in the long run you will save money because natural fabrics wear longer than synthetics. They also allow the air to pass through them, making them much more comfortable. They look a lot better, too.

# *Shopping*

Shopping for clothes is just like shopping for anything else: it's easier if you know what you're looking for. If you go into a grocery store armed with a shopping list, you will spend less and get everything you need. We all know that the worst time to shop for groceries is when we're hungry. It is just as true that the worst time to shop for a specific item — a blouse, a skirt, a coat — is when you need it for an interview or a meeting with a client tomorrow. Never shop when you're pressured and rushed or you're likely to overspend and wind up with something you'll never wear again.

Instead, know your wardrobe, know your needs, and buy the things that suit you whenever you find them. Get into the habit of buying clothes on sale, out of season. Once you've made some good buys, you'll resent paying the full price ever again.

There are some stores that specialize in selling clothes at a discount. Generally, they fall into two types: the stores that sell low-quality merchandise and the stores that sell high-quality merchandise. Stores like Loehmann's (found in the East and in Los Angeles) which sell good clothes at reduced prices are the salvation of working women, but K-Mart and Zayre's have their uses too — go there for underwear, stockings, and make-up.

Factory outlets exist all over the country. The town of Reading, Pennsylvania, has become a bargain hunter's mecca because of its many factory outlets.

Don't be afraid to shop in expensive shops. After their clothes are marked down, they can be as reasonable as clothes of lower quality in less expensive stores. Certain high-fashion shops have special departments for end-of-the-line sale items from all their departments. Bonwit Teller's Finale Shop no longer exists, unfortunately, but when in Joseph Magnin's, head right for the Magnarama Shop, and in Boston, look in Filene's basement before shopping anywhere else.

Here are some general shopping tips:

1. Make out a shopping list at home. Do you need a sweater? Don't leave the house without a list of the colors of each skirt, blazer, and pair of pants you'd like to wear it with.

2. Try to avoid shopping at lunch time.

3. Shop first in stores that have given you satisfaction in

104

the past. Look for designers whose clothes have given you pleasure and good wear.

4. Don't shop with a friend. She travels fastest who travels alone.

5. Buy the best clothes you can afford. Buy fewer items, if you must, but always try to buy quality. It will pay off in good looks and durability.

6. Always buy the most important item in your ensemble first. In other words, buy the suit before you buy the blouse.

# Role Models

Imitation is more than the sincerest form of flattery. It is one of the easiest ways to put together a look you like. Always keep your eyes open for women who are projecting an image of success. Don't be afraid to go up to a well-dressed woman in the street and ask where she bought her outfit or who did her hair. She'll be delighted and you'll be on your way.

When you see a woman you admire in the office or in a magazine or even in a movie, look again. What is she wearing? What is it about her that makes her look special?

You can get ideas on how to look and what to wear just by turning on your television. Jane Pauley and Barbara Walters are usually dressed like successful businesswomen, and Mary Tyler Moore's classic clothes are as up-to-date today in reruns as they were when she originally played a Minneapolis television executive.

# 8

# *Body Perfection: Shape Up for Success* _____

Just because you sit at a desk all day is no reason to look as if you do. No outfit, no matter how well cut and well designed, will look as good on a woman who is out of shape as it will on a woman who is trim and fit. And the only way to become trim and fit and stay that way is to eat sensibly and to exercise. If you are out of shape, you will be surprised at how quickly your body will respond to attention and care. Just fifteen minutes a day can work wonders.

In order to determine your ideal weight, first you must define your body type. To do so, pull a tape measure tightly around your wrist. If your wrist measures less than six inches around, your frame is small. If your wrist measures six inches around, you have a medium frame, and if it is more than six inches, you have a large frame.

The table below indicates approximate "ideal" weights for women. If you wish to retain a healthy figure, no matter how old you are, your weight should stay as close to the ideal as possible. Weigh and measure yourself without shoes or clothes.

## IDEAL WEIGHTS BY HEIGHT

| HEIGHT | SMALL FRAME | MEDIUM FRAME | LARGE FRAME |
|---|---|---|---|
| 5' | 100 | 105 | 110 |
| 5'1 | 105 | 110 | 115 |
| 5'2 | 110 | 115 | 120 |
| 5'3 | 115 | 120 | 125 |
| 5'4 | 120 | 125 | 130 |
| 5'5 | 125 | 130 | 135 |
| 5'6 | 130 | 135 | 140 |
| 5'7 | 135 | 140 | 145 |
| 5'8 | 140 | 145 | 150 |
| 5'9 | 145 | 150 | 155 |
| 5'10 | 150 | 155 | 160 |
| 5'11 | 155 | 160 | 165 |
| 6' | 160 | 170 | 170 |

Of course, it is possible to weigh your ideal weight, or even to weigh less, and still be out of shape. Every woman needs exercise for proper muscle tone. It is important to select an exercise program you can live with — anything too ambitious could set you off exercising forever. Try to select two or three exercises you enjoy doing and set aside a few minutes a day to devote to them. Scissor-kicks, sit-ups, jogging, and jumping rope all work, so do whatever is easiest and most enjoyable for you. But remember, exercise is only beneficial if you do it *regularly*.

# Posture

Clothes alone won't give you the executive look. Your every gesture is important in projecting your business image. Never underestimate the power of positive posture. Keep your head up, shoulders back, chest out, and tummy and fanny tucked in. And when you sit at your desk, sit up straight. Efficiency of movement and the elimination of wasted energy are important in projecting the image we want others to have of us.

# Exercise for Relaxation — at Work and at Home

Tension can be a real obstacle to success. Since most of us are not experienced yogis with perfect control over our thoughts and actions, it helps to know some exercises that can be done in times of stress during business hours. Perhaps you have an important meeting coming up. Before you go, take a few minutes in the privacy of your office to run through these simple foot exercises, which you may do while sitting at your desk. You don't even have to take your shoes off!

1. Cross one leg over the opposite knee and circle the ankle twenty times clockwise, then twenty times counter-clockwise. Now, reverse your legs and do the other ankle.

2. Raise both feet off the floor with the knees straight and the legs slightly apart. Holding onto the seat of your chair for support, rotate both feet in toward each other, then out away from each other, then both to the left, then both to the right. Do each rotation ten times for a total of forty.

3. Leaving your left foot on the floor, kick your right leg up until your leg is straight. Kick high, lifting your thigh off the chair and pointing your toes back toward your knee so that you can feel the muscles pull. Kick ten times for each leg.

To relax your whole body, try letting it go limp all over. Nothing is more relaxing. If you can lie down for a few minutes during the day, you'll be surprised at how refreshed you will feel. If this is impossible, go limp in your chair, leaning backward or folded forward (do this when no one is looking!). in either case, let your arms dangle loosely at your sides.

## ACHING NECK AND SHOULDERS
This can be a real problem for anyone who sits at a desk for hours at a time. If you don't feel your best, you won't look your best. Here are some exercises that will help you look and feel better without getting up from your desk:

1. Stretch toward the sky. Double your fists and push

upward, pushing the tension in your shoulder muscles up and away.

2. Place your right hand on your right shoulder and your left hand on your left shoulder. Bring your shoulders forward as far as they will go, up toward your ears, then back down and as far back as they will go. Do this front-and-back motion ten times.

3. Clasp your hands behind your head and pull your elbows back as far as they will go. Inhale as you pull them back, exhale as you relax.

4. To relieve neck strain, let your jaw drop open relaxed and rotate your head slowly in a circle. Do this several times whenever you feel tension mounting in your neck.

## TIRED LEGS

Standing in one place is more tiring than walking because the blood is not stimulated to rush through the vessels to replenish the muscle cells. A good remedy for tired legs is the toning bath.

Just before going to bed at night, get into a bathtub that has just enough warm water in it to cover your legs. Using a good, stiff hand brush, start with your feet and ankles and scrub all the way up to the tops of your thighs. Rub gently at first until the skin is pink and tingling. Then turn on the cold water and sit until the water is cool enough to drive the blood from the surface of your skin. Then get quickly out of the tub, blot yourself dry, and get into bed.

## HEADACHE AND EYE STRAIN

You can sometimes stop a headache and relieve eye strain by gently massaging the temples with the three main fingers, allowing the thumbs to rest just under the cheek bones. The fingertips are rotated over a small area and then moved slightly until the whole area around the eyes has been massaged.

The mind tenses the muscles of the jaw as you think. The more emotional your thoughts, the tighter the jaw becomes. To relax these muscles, massage behind and just in front of the ear. Use a slight amount of pressure.

Here are some other exercises for both strengthening and relaxing the muscles in your eyes and face:

1. Hold your head erect. Place your chin in the heels of the palms and let your hands hold your head in place. Without moving your head, look up and then down. Continue shifting your eyes steadily up and down for several counts. This exercise stretches and strengthens the vertical eye muscles.

2. Exercise the horizontal eye muscles by slowly looking as far from side to side as possible. Hold your head still. Now close your eyes for a moment and relax.

3. Cup your right hand over your right eye and your left hand over your left eye, letting the heels of your hands rest on your cheekbones. Do not put pressure on the eye ball. Close your eyes.

4. Holding your head erect with your hands holding the head still, look straight ahead and blink once. Look straight up, where twelve o'clock would be on a huge clock, blink five times, look straight ahead and blink once. Continue around the clock, to the right upper corner, the right side, the right lower corner, straight down, and so on. Blink five times at each position and blink once as you look straight ahead between each position.

5. Squeeze your eyes shut, and tightly contract all the muscles of your mouth and face. Make your face as small as you can. Now open the eyes wide, open the mouth, raise the eyebrows. Repeat about five times.

112

# What's Your Line

Assuming your figure can use some camouflage, the following is a list of dos and don'ts for the four major figure types:

## *TALL* ―――――――――――――――――――――――――

### *WEAR*

Horizontal lines — wide belts, yoke lines, circular trimming.

Hip-length or three-quarter-length blazers.

Contrasting colors.

Large accessories, bulky jewelry, large handbags.

Soft, rounded shoulders.

Naturally textured fabrics, nubby wools.

Bulky knits.

A-line, dirndl, and gored skirts.

*AVOID*

Pencil lines, narrow belts.

Vertically placed tucks or buttons.

Medium-length blazers.

Angular trimming, contour pleats.

Exaggerated shoulders.

Tightly fitted, full-length sleeves.

Flimsy fabrics, small patterns.

Tight, straight skirts.

## SHORT

### WEAR ─────────────────────────────────

Vertical lines from neck to hem.

Short jackets.

Easy-fitting sleeves, full-length or short.

Small accessories, small pieces of jewelry, and small handbags.

Soft, lightweight fabrics, such as wool gabardine and silk.

Self-belts or no belt.

Medium-full skirts (no wider than A-line).

Simplicity in detail.

*AVOID*

Horizontal lines, all exaggerated lines.

Overlong blazers.

Sleeves chopped at the elbow.

Massive trimming, such as a large belt buckle.

Bulky furs, bulky fabrics.

Large plaids and prints.

Wide cuffs.

Wide or contrasting belts.

Box pleats.

Conspicuous hems, contrasting borders.

Lines that break up the body.

---

## *HEAVY*

### *WEAR*

Vertical lines, center panels, buttons down the front.

Simple dresses with half-belts.

Medium-weight fabrics.

Diagonal trimming, such as pockets.

Medium-gored skirts with center stitching or pleat.

Set-in sleeves.

V-necklines and point collars.

Blazers not longer than two inches below the hipbone.

Narrow self-belts.

*AVOID*

Horizontal lines, round necks and collars.

Two-piece dresses.

Clinging or heavy fabrics.

Curved lines.

Skirts with all-around pleats or wide gores.

Puffy, droopy, or tightly fitted sleeves.

Very long or short blazers.

Set-in belts, wide or contrasting belts.

---

## THIN _____

### WEAR

Horizontal and curved lines.

Two-piece dresses and suits.

Full-bodied fabrics.

Large pockets modified according to height.

Dull-finish skirts.

Small and thin? Wear small accessories.

Tall and thin? Wear large accessories.

Soft, rounded shoulders with easy-fitting sleeves.

*AVOID*

Vertical lines, exaggerated lines.

Deep V-necklines.

Tight-fitting clothes.

Clinging, flimsy fabrics.

Pencil-slim skirts.

Exaggerated shoulders.

Tight sleeves.

---

# 9

*The When
and Where of
Successful Dressing:
Tailoring
Your Clothes
for the Occasion
and Locale* _____

# *Business Entertaining*

So you have to take a client out to dinner. Now what do you wear? You don't want to come on like a lady of the evening, of course, yet you don't want to look cold and distant, either. Business entertaining, while still business, should be fun.

Your outfit should be more feminine and more stylish than something you'd wear to the office. Dressing up is one way to tell your client that he — or she — is special, and that your dinner together is a special occasion.

What should you wear? Nothing seductive or far-out. After all, this is still business. You can turn heads on your own time.

# *Chairing a Meeting*

Color psychology is the key to dressing to speak before a group. Does speaking in public make you feel insecure? If you need to project an extra measure of authority, by all means, bring out the big guns. Get into your most tailored navy or gray suit. Keep away from frills and pastels. Wearing a tailored, white blouse under your jacket will make you look as if you were born to be in charge.

On the other hand, if you already feel comfortable about the group you'll be addressing, and if your concern is making them accept *you,* include a warm color in your outfit. Wearing a beige or blue skirt with an apricot or soft yellow blouse will give you a look of relaxed confidence and invite a favorable response. When fashion expert Emily Cho appeared on the *Today* show, she wore a lavender wool dress with soft but tailored lines

124

because she felt anything severe would intimidate her audience. Don't let your clothes intimidate your audience unless you've planned it that way.

# A Regional Dress Guide

Will the same outfit that works in Portland, Oregon, work in Portland, Maine? The outfit that a junior executive might wear in one part of the country might be more appropriate for the typing pool in another. Women who work for corporations in New York City and throughout the Northeast are generally very sophisticated in their dress. They seem to have an infallible sense of high fashion. If you intend to work in the East, it would make sense to study fashion in books and magazines to develop such a sense. Conservative colors and basic, tailored clothes work well in the Northeast. Gray, brown, navy, and black look sophisticated and are easy to build a wardrobe around. Women who work in the Northeast rarely wear white shoes (in fact, they claim that white shoes are a sure way to spot an out-of-towner in the city), and you should follow their lead and rely on bone and other neutral colors for summer shoes.

In the South, women in business wear more colors and more patterns, and male employees accept it as a natural thing. White is considered smart for shoes and bags.

Large cities in the Midwest demand the same sophistication found in the Northeast, although this sophistication is interpreted more conservatively with less emphasis on high fashion. Classically tailored clothes are as perfect in Chicago as they are in New York.

Throughout the West, clothes in general and specifically women's work clothes can be more flamboyant and much more easygoing. California's businesswomen have a casual chic all

125

their own. A woman would not dream of wearing a straw wedgie to work in Detroit, but on the West Coast shoes like that would not detract from a female executive's serious image. In the Southwestern states, such as Texas and Oklahoma, women are not as casual as they are in California, but neither are they as conservative as they are in the East. A tailored shirtdress in a warm yellow color would look right at home at a business meeting in Phoenix or in an executive suite in Houston. If you travel on the job, remember to adjust your wardrobe accordingly.

# Sales Conferences

Sales conferences in city locales call for the same dress you'd normally wear to work. However, many sales meetings are now held at resorts where casual dress is more common. Don't let tennis or beach wear carry over to the conference room. Stay away from braless, low cut sports wear and short shorts. Good slacks and shirts, or perhaps a peasant skirt and shawl, are comfortable, informal outfits that won't cut your business credibility.

# When You're Out of the Office

Many women spend a great deal of their days visiting clients, attending out-of-the-office meetings, meeting buyers — anywhere but behind their desks. You must pay special attention to your coat, shoes or boots, handbag, briefcase, and gloves. You needn't dress much differently from the woman who spends her entire day inside her office, but you should choose clothes that can be worn easily under your coat. In mild weather, an all-purpose blazer looks smashing over a shirt dress, and will keep you comfortable and elegant all over town.

# *The Interview*

We form impressions of people within thirty seconds after meeting them. In a job interview, you must make the first thirty seconds count. What you wear depends on the kind of job you're seeking, the company you'll join, and the interviewer you'll talk to.

If you are a recent college graduate looking for a management-training position, your appearance must compensate for your lack of experience. Wearing a navy or gray suit and sensible shoes will give you a more experienced look. Youth and inexperience are not a handicap — everybody was young once — but corporations will favor young people who carry themselves with *confidence*.

A mature, experienced woman looking for a job must take a different approach. Wearing beige or pale gray, for instance, would give a woman a look of competence without being threatening. If these colors are not flattering to your coloring, wear them with a blouse or scarf in a shade more complimentary to your skin tone. In fact, accessories worn next to your face should always be in soft, flattering colors. When meeting an unknown interviewer in unfamiliar territory, however, it is more important than ever to wear neutral colors.

If you are interviewing for another job within your own company, choosing your outfit should be much easier. Just re-read the dress suggestions for your type and try for the most capable look you can present.

Neutral colors will also work for the mature woman who is seeking employment for the first time, or for the first time in many years. You want to look knowledgeable and capable, not like a homemaker. Do wear classic, tailored clothes even if you have to go out and buy them for your interview. *Do not* wear a pastel polyester pants suit.

Here are some general interviewing tips:

1. Greet the interviewer by name as you enter the office. If necessary, check the pronunciation with the receptionist.

2. Unless you are looking for a job in sales, shake hands only if the interviewer makes the first move. If you are looking for a sales position, assertiveness and aggressiveness are part of the job, and you will be expected to offer your hand immediately.

3. Wait to sit down until a chair is offered and never sit down before your interviewer has been seated.

4. Don't smoke, regardless of what your interviewer does.

5. Do your homework and know as much about the company you want to work for as possible, so that you can ask an intelligent question or two.

6. Be definite about what job you're after.

# 10

## Report from the Front Lines_____

How do women really dress on the job? Here's the word from seven women *and* men:

*Sarah McClendon*
*White House Correspondent*
*Washington, D.C.*

Newspaper women have the reputation of looking dowdy and, I'm afraid, in many cases, that reputation is well-deserved. Few women in journalism pay much attention to their appearance. They are not paid well enough to be able to afford expensive clothes, and they are too busy to make the most of what they do have. I work with women who believe that wearing makeup is morally inferior and beneath them.

After thirty years as a newspaper reporter, though, I have decided that personal appearance is very important, and now I spend much more time and money on clothes and makeup than I ever did when I was younger. Now when I dress to go to a nationally-televised presidential press conference, for instance, I use color psychology when I plan my outfit. I've learned that wearing light colors makes me look washed out, unimportant and uninteresting. On the other hand, wearing bright colors makes people notice me. I feel good (and I think look good) in a green wool dress I bought because of its strong, yet soothing, color. When I wore it to a White House press conference, President Carter called on me for the first time in over a year.

*Richard P. Toft*
*Vice President, Lincoln National Life Insurance Company*
*Fort Wayne, Indiana*

The women in management positions at Lincoln National Life do not dress with the same flair as the more "with it" secretaries. They are less responsive to fads and fashion. I believe that these women are making concessions to how they *think* they should look in the eyes of male senior staff. As far as I know, though, and I've worked with more women executives than any other man in our office, dress has never been a consideration when senior staff evaluates a woman's performance on the job.

*Cheryl Beil*
*Assistant Dean of Students, George Washington University*
*Washington, D.C.*

Women on the faculty of our business school usually come here to teach after spending a few years as young executives in the business world. They are what I call "uniform dressers," so into the dress for success mold that they wear suits every day and never take off their jackets.

On the other hand, academics break all the rules when it comes to dressing. Even the men don't wear suits. With the exception of the business school faculty, many of our teachers never worked at a "real" job. They tend to dress informally, to say the least, and some of them dress as informally as their students. Most of the younger men and women wear jeans.

As a member of the university's administration, I never wear jeans or slacks. I try to look my best, which means wearing a dress, when I meet with the president of the university, or when I am attending any function also attended by the students' parents. When I meet with students, however, I try to look more casual. I think they are more comfortable with me when I am dressed in a skirt and blouse or a skirt and sweater.

*Michael Koleda*
*Executive Director, The President's Commission on Coal*
*Washington, D.C.*

On Capitol Hill, congressional offices are terribly cramped. They are tiny, and tend to be overcrowded with desks, files, and office staff. Women who work in these offices find that it just isn't worth it to dress well. The staff offices of congressmen are closer to a warehouse than they are to the White House when it comes to decor and ambiance. It would look silly if the women who work for congressmen wore clothes that are grander than their surroundings.

Women who work for a senator, on the other hand, are better dressed. They are expected to look good. It's part of the whole senatorial image.

Women who work in the White House wear the dressiest clothes of all. I have never seen any woman in the West Wing dressed in a pants suit. They wear dresses or suits, and their clothes look expensive and tasteful. They tend to wear jewelry — beads and earrings — and they are always perfectly groomed.

*Carol Kaganov*
*Creative Chief, Sales Promotion, Avon Products*
*New York, New York*

Most of the women I work with, both the secretaries and the executives, dress well in everything from well-cut and well-tailored blue jeans to skirts and blazers. The women being promoted aren't necessarily the ones who look best, but I've found that women who wear sloppy or inappropriate clothes are often displaying (whether consciously or unconsciously) an anti-corporate attitude that carries over to other areas of their work. These women are seldom promoted. In general, though, this corporation sees through clothes to the people underneath, and women and men who work here are successful because of the work they do, not the clothes they wear.

*Bill Brown*
*Producer, NBC News*
*New York, New York*

At NBC, everyone has a sense of upward mobility, and they dress accordingly. It is really impossible, at least in the news division, to tell which women are secretaries and which ones are associate producers just by looking at them. If a woman making $8,000 a year has the wit to dress tastefully, she is going to look better than a woman making $20,000 a year with no taste. Both women and men at NBC News wear a whole range of outfits from dungarees to suits and ties and dresses. We work behind the scenes, and what we wear doesn't matter as much as the quality of our work. Talent is what counts in television.

*Dana Lichty*
*Executive Director, Riverdale Neighborhood House*
*Riverdale, New York*

I can wear almost anything to work, but not everyday. I can wear jeans or a skirt and sweater on the days when I'm going to be in the office, meeting with my staff. If I'm going to be around children, which is a large part of what we do here, I wear jeans.

But if I'm going to the Ford Foundation to ask for a grant, I wear a tailored suit. I try to look really good, but not *rich*. I would never wear designer clothes or jewelry. People are not supposed to get rich from the social services, and a high fashion image could turn people off.

## Your Personal Style

Clearly, women all over the country have adopted a wide variety of clothing styles. Some tailor their clothes to their occupation, some wear what they're "expected" to wear, and some use clothes to make a personal statement of who they are and what they believe. The most important thing to remember is the old adage, "to thine own self be true." Study the different types presented in this book and pick your own. Then you can begin telling the true story about yourself through your clothes.

The clothes you wear are very much a statement of your inner confidence as well as your life style. When you hide behind a uniform, you're saying to the world, "I have no confidence in my own taste."

You *can* be well dressed and maintain a professional, promotable image without sacrificing the little details that mark you as different from the rest. Be a little adventuresome in your business dress, and you'll stand out as an individual, a leader — someone who's really going places!